WHICH NATIVE FERN?

New Zealand Native Ferns — A Simple Guide
to their Identification, Ecology and Uses

ANDREW CROWE

PENGUIN BOOKS

Introduction to Ecology Edition

Walk into any New Zealand forest and you will find ferns. Indeed, among temperate lands, this country has such a wealth and variety of them that it is known as 'The Land of Ferns'. In size, these ancient flowerless plants range from the giant mamaku tree fern, which can rise to the height of a five-storey building, down to the most delicate filmy ferns, some smaller than a fingernail. The number of species found in this country is almost 200. This book aims to help the reader to confidently identify the most common and striking of them.

New Information in the Nature Notes

Since the original *Which?* books were written, there has been a huge growth of interest in New Zealand's native plants, with many now being widely grown in gardens. This has brought with it a fresh appreciation of the country's ecology and the problems posed, for example, by possums. Hence, the response of this new edition is to explore nature's interconnectedness more fully. Readers may be surprised to learn that ferns play an important part in the lives of many creatures of the forest: not only native birds and introduced possums, goats, deer and pigs, but also insects. Some of the specialist fern-eating caterpillars can be conspicuous, particularly the fern leaf-tyers and fern loopers.

◀ Left, a **Fern Leaf-Tyer** [Family: Tortricidae] The caterpillars of these moths use webbing to tie fronds together as a retreat from which to safely feed on the fern. This distinctive home-making tactic helps the caterpillar avoid being eaten by birds (and wasps).

Right, a **Fern Looper** [Family: Geometridae] ▶ The caterpillars of these moths have a rather comical way of walking, forming a high loop between each step. They are usually found on the underside of fronds, often feeding more actively at night – again, a tactic for avoiding being eaten by birds.

Many of both kinds of caterpillars are specialists. That is, most will eat nothing else but the fronds of ferns, with many kinds feeding on just one or two species. These caterpillars will develop into adult moths, most of them native. As adult moths, they will fly mostly at night, roaming the forest by moonlight and/or by scent in search of white or pale-coloured flowers to feed on their nectar, frequently providing a pollination service in the process. There are also tiny, fern leafminer flies here, whose maggots tunnel within the fronds, and fern whitefly species that leave white wax on the fronds, too. However, this book does not attempt to list every invertebrate known to feed on each fern. It is an introduction only. To explore further, refer to the Crop & Food Research invertebrate herbivore–host plant association Plant-SyNZ™ database website: **http://plant-synz.landcareresearch.co.nz**

New Information on Māori Names

The background to much of the information on Māori names constitutes part of another much longer-term project – see page 62.

Using this Book

For simplicity this book tries to keep to words that are part of everyday language.

Frond – the leaf of a fern (including its stalk)
Leaflet – the smallest division of a frond
Spore – the dust-like 'seed' of a fern

A few simple points about using these frond keys

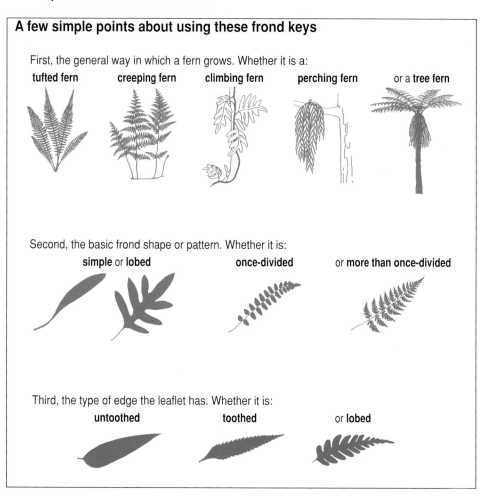

First, the general way in which a fern grows. Whether it is a:

tufted fern   **creeping fern**   **climbing fern**   **perching fern**   or a **tree fern**

Second, the basic frond shape or pattern. Whether it is:

simple or **lobed**   **once-divided**   or **more than once-divided**

Third, the type of edge the leaflet has. Whether it is:

untoothed   **toothed**   or **lobed**

To use the frond keys

1. Find a typical frond of a common adult fern, but don't pull it off because you'll need to examine how it grows on the fern. Now turn to page 5. Starting at the bottom of the chart, turn to the page indicated.

2. From the arrow at the bottom of this new page, follow the appropriate branches until you arrive at an illustration of your frond. Now turn to the page indicated for a photograph of the fern and a frond silhouette.

3. Check your identification by running down the checklist next to the photograph and compare the sketch showing the way in which the fern grows and how big it gets.

Understanding the fern pages

Ferns that look similar appear on facing pages. The identification checklists on these pages help distinguish between them. The following graphics are there to help:

A guide to the approximate range over which the wild fern is usually found. ▶

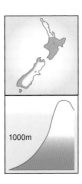

A guide to the altitudes where the fern naturally grows (in metres). ▶

The common shape, habit and height of the mature fern. An adult person or a copy of this book are alongside to help with scale. ▼

Beneath the colour photo you'll find a life-sized silhouette of part of the frond and, in some cases, a life-sized photo of a section of the underneath of a frond to show how the spore cases are arranged on that particular fern.*

Common names

It is often said that Māori named only those plants useful to them, simply inventing the rest to please curious Pākehā; this theory has been very effectively put to the test. In 1834, Austrian botanist Baron von Hügel made a collection of 300 plants and asked one Māori man to name them. Though many of the plants were small and apparently insignificant, he named them all. The following evening another man was invited to do the same. He, too, named all 300. All but one plant received the same name as had been given the night before.

Names (whether Māori or not) do, however, vary from region to region. In acknowledgement of the fact that the name used by one tribe is no more valid than another, you will find several fern names in this book. Those not found in *A Dictionary of the Maori Language* (Williams) were mostly supplied to H. B. Dobbie some time prior to 1930 by Edward Joseph, Bethlehem, Tauranga.**

As a guide to correct pronunciation, Māori vowels are sounded as follows: 'a' as in 'far', 'e' as in 'bet', 'i' as in 'me', 'o' as in 'or', 'u' as in 'flu'. Macrons have been included and these indicate a lengthened vowel, e.g. ā = aa, thus Māori = Maaori.

---

* Indeed, the arrangement of these 'spore cases' (or patches) is so central to fern identification that it will later become necessary to appreciate that these 'spore cases' or 'spore patches' are, in fact, *sori*. A sorus consists of many tiny brown capsules, called *sporangia*. It is in these sporangia that the microscopic spores (usually 64 spores per sporangia) are contained. A protective flap called an *indusium* often covers and protects the sorus.

** Where a choice exists between Māori names, I have generally used those favoured by James Beever (see references). Those not listed by Beever are either from Dobbie (3rd edition) or Potts, T. H. *Out in the Open*.

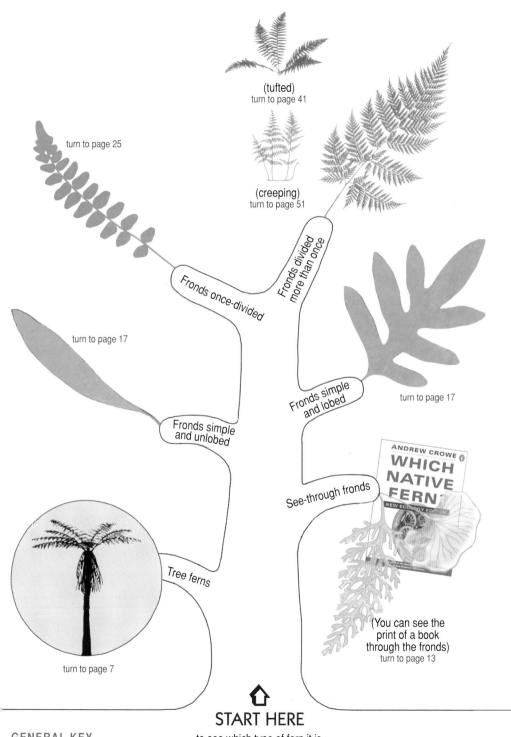

(tufted)
turn to page 41

(creeping)
turn to page 51

turn to page 25

Fronds divided more than once

Fronds once-divided

turn to page 17

Fronds simple and lobed

turn to page 17

Fronds simple and unlobed

ANDREW CROWE
WHICH NATIVE FERN
NEW ECOLOGY ED

See-through fronds

Tree ferns

(You can see the print of a book through the fronds)
turn to page 13

turn to page 7

⌂
START HERE

GENERAL KEY   to see which type of fern it is

5

Mamaku
Black Tree Fern

*Cyathea medullaris** [Family: Cyatheaceae]

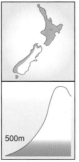

Size: Trunk up to 20 m tall; *fronds up to 5 m*

Features: Tree fern with *flattish oval frond scars* on the trunk. *Frond stalks black and very thick.* Fronds arching. Dead fronds mostly fall but can form an untidy skirt, especially on young plants.

Where: Common in damp forest gullies. Native to New Zealand and several Pacific Islands

'Mamaku' is a traditional tree-fern name from tropical east Polynesia. The white pith of the trunk and branches was an important Māori food but is very slimy until steamed in a hāngi. The flavour improves with drying. Also used as a poultice for sores and wounds, and the reddish gum taken internally for worms and diarrhoea. Matted aerial roots at the base of the trunk were split into slabs as a rat-proof lining for kūmara pits. New Zealand's tallest tree fern. Known overseas as **sago fern**.

Nature Notes: Birds collect loose brown scales (photo, top) on new growth as nesting material. 'Fiddleheads' and white pith eaten by possums. Young fronds are webbed together by caterpillars of the native 'brownheaded leafroller' moth (*Ctenopseustis herana*) – photo below – while holes in them are made by a small, light-brown, native 'fern leaf beetle'. Inside dead fronds live at least three kinds of weevil grubs. Trees are apparently being killed by a phytoplasma disease.

Growing It: Easy; fast-growing. Water in dry weather; shelter from wind and frost.

LIFE SIZE

*Also known as *Sphaeropteris medullaris*.

6

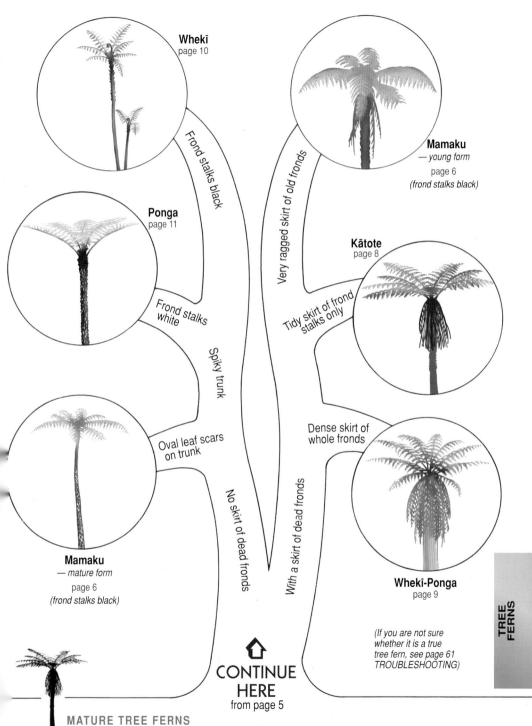

Whekī
page 10

Mamaku
— *young form*
page 6
(frond stalks black)

Ponga
page 11

Kātote
page 8

Frond stalks black

Very ragged skirt of old fronds

Tidy skirt of frond stalks only

Frond stalks white

Spiky trunk

Oval leaf scars on trunk

Dense skirt of whole fronds

No skirt of dead fronds

With a skirt of dead fronds

Mamaku
— *mature form*
page 6
(frond stalks black)

Whekī-Ponga
page 9

(If you are not sure whether it is a true tree fern, see page 61 TROUBLESHOOTING)

⌂
CONTINUE
HERE
from page 5

**TREE
FERNS**

MATURE TREE FERNS
The skirts of dead fronds will depend also on how sheltered the tree fern is.

7

Kātote
Soft Tree Fern

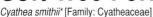

Cyathea smithii* [Family: Cyatheaceae]

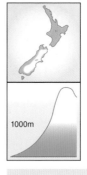

1000m

Size: Trunk up to 8 m tall; fronds to 2.5 m

Features: Tree fern with very *soft, pale horizontal fronds*. Older trees wear a *short skirt of dried stalks that hang like giant stick insects*

Where: Common in colder and wetter forests, especially at higher altitudes and in the far south. Native only to New Zealand

The world's southernmost tree fern – found even on the Auckland Islands. Also known as **whē** (meaning 'stick insect'). South Island Māori ate the cooked heart, which Herries Beattie described in 1920 as 'a good feed [that] might make good jam'. In 1847, however, Brunner (perhaps referring to the *raw* heart) described it as 'far from palatable, and exceedingly indigestible'. Kātote has the chemical ability to reduce the root growth of competing plants.

Nature Notes: Kererū (New Zealand pigeons) nibble the fronds. Kōtuku (white herons) collect frond stalks to build nest platforms. In spring, the caterpillars of at least four kinds of fern leaf-tyer moths and two fern loopers feed on the fronds. Eaten by possums but seldom by goats.

Growing It: Grows best where moist and cold but needs shelter from wind and frost when young. Otherwise hardy.

LIFE SIZE

Photos (top): 'kātote ugly nestmaker' (left) and 'oblique-waved fern looper' moth and caterpillar (centre and right).

* Also known as *Alsophila smithii*.

Wheki-Ponga
Dicksonia fibrosa [Family: Dicksoniaceae]

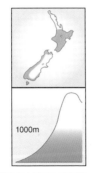

1000m

Size: Trunk up to 6 m tall; fronds 1.5–3 m long

Features: Tree fern with *very thick, soft, fibrous, rusty-brown trunk*. Many narrow fronds on very short stalks, *harsh* to touch. Old trees wear a very thick, *dense skirt* of dead fronds

Where: In forest and semi-open country. Native only to New Zealand

This is probably the slowest-growing New Zealand tree fern, with many specimens several hundred years old. The thick trunk consists largely of aerial roots. The fibre in these trunks is so remarkably hard that it is tough-eating, even for rodents. Indeed, in some areas, Māori split these fibrous trunks into hard slabs for lining buildings, especially food stores. The 'fat tree fern'.

Nature Notes: Several species of caterpillars feed on the fronds, including at least five kinds of native leaf-tyer moths and one fern looper. Unlike other tree ferns, the unusually dense skirt of old fronds stops the trunk from being used as a foothold for perching plants.

Growing It: More tolerant of sun and wind than most tree ferns, but keep the roots protected from drying out and protect the tree from the drying effects of wind and sun by not removing dead fronds.

Photo (top): 'tiger bell moth', whose caterpillars web the fronds together.

LIFE SIZE

TREE FERNS

9

Whekī
Rough Tree Fern

Dicksonia squarrosa [Family: Dicksoniaceae]

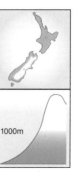

1000m

Size:	Up to 7 m tall; fronds 1.5–3 m
Features:	Tree fern with slender, often *branching*, trunk covered with *black, peg-like remains of fallen fronds*. Few fronds, scratchy to touch, spreading almost horizontally. The dead fronds generally fall off to leave no skirt
Where:	Very common in forest. Native only to New Zealand

Whekī is a traditional tree-fern name from east Polynesia. Because the trunks last well in the ground, Māori used them to build fences and house walls. For decorative effect, the outer surface would be hewn clean to show the internal patterning. These would sometimes be interspersed with panels of fern stalks or reeds. Until very recently, the trunks were also being laid along swampy sections of forest tracks. The fronds have proven antiviral properties against influenza type A.

Nature Notes: Fronds eaten by kererū (pigeons) and deer. The peg-like remains of old fronds on the trunk offer crevices for soil to form – a good foothold for perching plants. Two kinds of weevil live inside the dead trunks, and five leafroller caterpillars inside webbing on the fronds.

Growing It: The only common tree fern capable of sprouting from buried pieces of trunk. Also spreads from underground runners, sometimes forming whole colonies. Tolerates sun and some wind; roots benefit from mulching. Hardy.

Photo (top): 'ginger ponga leaf-tyer' moth, whose caterpillars web the tips of fronds together.

LIFE SIZE

Ponga
Silver Tree Fern

*Cyathea dealbata** [Family: Cyatheaceae]

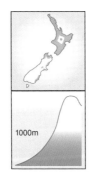

1000m

Size: Trunk up to 10 m tall; fronds up to 4 m long

Features: Tree fern with peg-like frond remains on the trunk. *Stalk and underside of mature fronds white* (not apparent until the fern is three or four years old)

Where: Common in dry forest and open scrub; rare on the west of the South Island. Native only to New Zealand

This is the emblem on All Black jerseys, its Māori name being a traditional tree-fern name from tropical Polynesia. Māori used the hard wood to make combs (kaponga) and the barbed points of bird spears and fish hooks. The fronds were used as soft matting on floors of sitting and sleeping rooms (silver side down, so as not to be annoyed by the spores). Placed silver side up, they serve as night-time track-markers, the orientation of the tips indicating direction

Nature Notes: Soil forming in crevices in the trunk provides a foothold for perching plants. Forest birds collect scales from the top of the trunk as nesting material. Among the many kinds of insects found on the fronds are a native 'fern leaf beetle', five kinds of leaf-tyer caterpillars, and three fern looper caterpillars. Native grubs of the 'fourspined weevil' are found in the dry, dead midribs. Dead stalks support a white 'ponga spore fungus'.

Growing It: Slow-growing but easy to establish in good, well-drained soil. Needs shelter from wind to look attractive.

LIFE SIZE

Photos (top): 'fourspined weevil' (left) and caterpillar and moth of the 'silver fern looper' (right).

* Also known as *Alsophila tricolor*.

TREE FERNS

11

Raurenga
Kidney Fern

Hymenophyllum nephrophyllum * [Family: Hymenophyllaceae]

Size:	Fronds 8–30 cm long
Features:	Creeping ground fern with *round to kidney-shaped, glossy, see-through,* *wavy-edged fronds on long, thin stalks.* Photo (top) shows mature frond
Where:	Forms mats on the forest floor, banks, rocks, or on tree trunks. Native only to New Zealand

One of New Zealand's most beautiful ferns. It often forms a delicate mat of fronds in which little else grows, something it achieves by producing a compound that – while allowing competing seeds to germinate – has the power to inhibit the growth of seedling roots. Another remarkable feature is its tolerance of dry summer conditions, when its fronds curl up tightly to avoid loss of moisture, yet recover fully very soon after rain. An alternative name, **kopakopa** (from to 'wrap or clasp'), describes this. The name 'raurenga' refers to the yellowish, translucent fronds, while 'kidney fern' describes their shape. This was a perfume plant of Māori, also worn in mourning.

Nature Notes: If you should find silk tubes attached to the fronds, these are likely to contain plump, green caterpillars of 'filmy-fern leaf-tyer' moths.

Growing It: Very difficult; does not transplant well and is not grown commercially. For the experts only in a glass case or purpose-built fernery.

LIFE SIZE

* Previously known as *Trichomanes reniforme.*

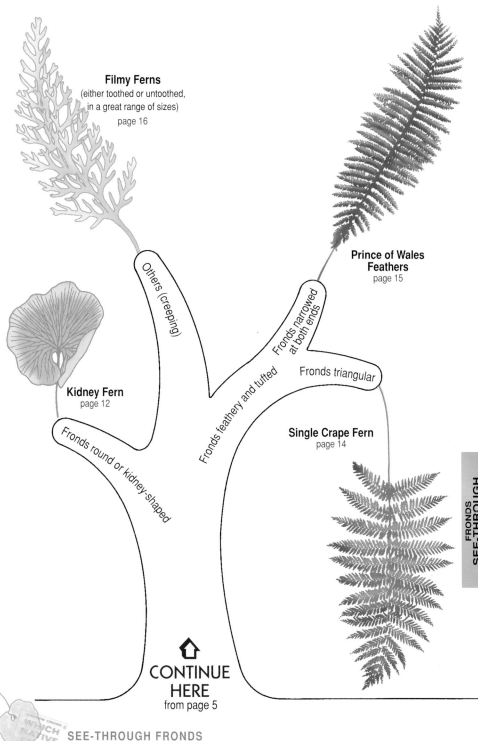

Filmy Ferns
(either toothed or untoothed, in a great range of sizes)
page 16

Others (creeping)

Prince of Wales Feathers
page 15

Fronds narrowed at both ends

Kidney Fern
page 12

Fronds feathery and tufted

Fronds triangular

Fronds round or kidney-shaped

Single Crape Fern
page 14

FRONDS
SEE-THROUGH

⌂
CONTINUE
HERE
from page 5

SEE-THROUGH FRONDS

13

Heruheru
Single Crape Fern

Leptopteris hymenophylloides [Family: Osmundaceae]

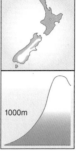

1000m

Size:	Trunk up to knee high; fronds 35–150 cm long
Features:	Tufted ground fern, often with a short woody trunk. Fronds very delicate, dark but *translucent* like a filmy fern, *finely divided but flat, and almost triangular*
Where:	Common in damp forest, especially by streams. Native only to New Zealand

At first glance, crape ferns look like filmy ferns for most of their fronds are likewise only one cell thick. However, on the underside of crape fern fronds, the spore capsules are scattered. There are two kinds of crape ferns, of which single crape fern is the more common. Its leaflets lie flat in one plane – hence the common name – distinguishing it from the more striking and delicate double crape fern, Prince of Wales feathers (opposite).

Nature Notes: In spring and summer, the bright green caterpillars (top right) of the 'pale fern looper' moth (female top left; male top centre) can sometimes be seen feeding on the undersides of fronds.

Growing It: This fern is not commercially available, because it is so difficult to emulate the correct conditions for it. Best propagated by spores and grown in a glass case or professional fernery with a sprinkler system.

LIFE SIZE

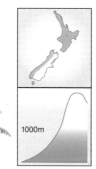

Heruheru
Prince of Wales Feathers

Leptopteris superba [Family: Osmundaceae]

1000m

Size:	Trunk up to waist high; fronds 25–100 cm long
Features:	Tufted ground fern, often with a short woody trunk. Fronds *tapered equally at both ends*, very finely divided. *Fluffy to touch.* Photo above shows underside of the mature frond
Where:	In wet forest, most commonly on the west of the South Island. Native only to New Zealand

One of New Zealand's favourite ferns, enjoyed for its remarkably delicate, feathery appearance. Most of the frond is just one cell thick, the finest divisions of the frond overlapping each other, standing up at right-angles to the frond, creating a wonderfully ornate feathery plume. The beauty of this effect is described by its common names, which include **crape fern** or **double crape fern** (sometimes spelt **crepe fern**). Māori likened the fronds to a comb ('heru'), coining many poetic alternative names for it, e.g. **ngutu kākāriki**, which likens the curved fronds to a parrot's beak.

Nature Notes: In spring and summer, the bright green caterpillars of the 'pale fern looper' moth are seen feeding on fronds. Also eaten by deer.

Growing It: Not grown commercially and difficult to maintain in good condition. Slow. Needs rich soil, constant dampness and cool conditions.

LIFE SIZE

FRONDS
SEE-THROUGH

15

Mauku Filmy Ferns

Hymenophyllum species [Family: Hymenophyllaceae]

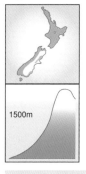

1500m

Size:	Fronds 8 mm–55 cm long, depending on the species
Features:	Several species, most creeping or perching with *thin, see-through fronds*. Mature frond shown below
Where:	Common in damp forest or high-rainfall areas, mostly on tree trunks, but also sometimes on rocks or on the ground. Most are native only to New Zealand

Mauku (or **mouku**) is a general Polynesian term for grasses and ferns used for animal feed or mulching of taro. New Zealand has almost 30 native filmy ferns – all with very thin fronds, many just one cell thick. Although they like damp bush or areas of high rainfall, most are able to cope with long periods of dry weather by curling up tightly. Several have strong chemical means of restricting the growth of competing plants.

Nature Notes: Silk tubes attached to some fronds may conceal plump, green caterpillars of about four species of 'filmy-fern leaf-tyer' moth that feed here. Kōkako (top centre) and kākāpō are known to eat the fronds, while kōkako and tīeke (saddlebacks) collect the fronds as nesting material.

Growing It:
Not commercially available. Require constantly humid conditions, a lot of shade and some ventilation. For this, either a glass case or a special fernery with sprinkler system is required.

LIFE SIZE

16

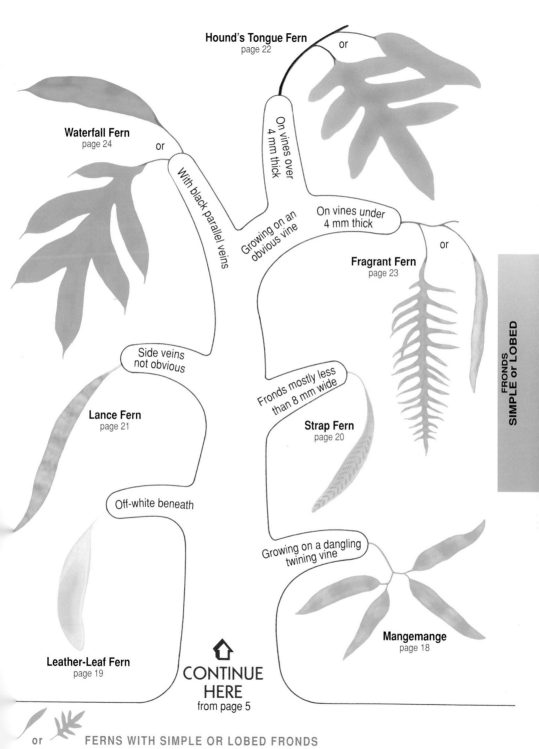

Hound's Tongue Fern
page 22

or

On vines over
4 mm thick

Waterfall Fern
page 24

or

With black parallel veins

On vines under
4 mm thick

Growing on an
obvious vine

Fragrant Fern
page 23

or

Side veins
not obvious

Lance Fern
page 21

Fronds mostly less
than 8 mm wide

Strap Fern
page 20

Off-white beneath

Growing on a dangling
twining vine

Mangemange
page 18

⬆
CONTINUE
HERE
from page 5

Leather-Leaf Fern
page 19

or   FERNS WITH SIMPLE OR LOBED FRONDS

Mangemange
Bushman's Mattress

Lygodium articulatum [Family: Lygodiaceae]

Size: Leaflets 4–10 cm long

Features: *Loosely climbing fern* with long, wiry, twisting stalks reaching into the tops of trees. Side stalks fork 2–3 times, ending in long, strap-like leaflets. Spore-bearing leaflets look like bunches of small green flowers

Where: Common in lowland forest. Native only to New Zealand

European settlers stuffed the corkscrew-like coils of climbing stems into bags to make a simple kind of spring-mattress – hence the name. Māori used these same stems as rope, for tying down thatch on huts, and to weave into fish-traps, inspiring an alternative name, **tarikupenga** ('snare-net'). Another name, **makamaka** (meaning 'to fish with hook and line'), would appear to refer to the fact that sections of vine that have curled around an obstacle, become so stiff that, when hardened by fire, they can be sharpened for use as fish-hooks. Technically speaking, the whole 'vine' from the ground up is one frond, so that mangemange (or **mangimangi**) can truly claim to have one of the longest leaves in the world.

Nature Notes: No specific insects on it are known.

Growing It: Does not transplant easily. Needs some shade and a support to climb. Difficult, but fast in warm areas.

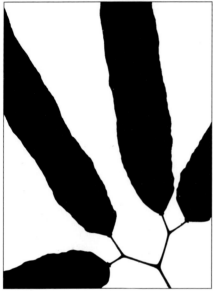

LIFE SIZE

Ngārara Wehi
Leather-Leaf Fern

Pyrrosia eleagnifolia [Family: Polypodiaceae]

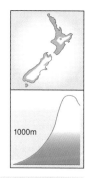

1000m

Size:	Fronds 3–20 cm long
Features:	Scrambling or climbing fern. Fronds thick and leathery, from long and tongue-like to almost round. *Underside pale and downy. Edges curled under*
Where:	Common on trees and rocks in native forest, exposed coasts and in gardens. Native only to New Zealand

The underside of the leaf-like fronds is clothed in a dense mat of fine hairs that appear under a microscope as pretty, star-like shapes, each only half a millimetre across. These and the fleshiness of the fronds help protect the fern from loss of water. Sister species in Australia are described as **felt ferns**. If derived from Tahitian, the Māori name could be translated as 'clothed in gecko'.

Nature Notes: Kōkako pluck pieces as nesting material. Two kinds of native caterpillar hide inside webbing on the fronds; another tunnels within them; three kinds hollow out the fronds. Fronds themselves are eaten by caterpillars (top right) of the 'hook-tip fern looper' moth. A brown 'witches broom' growth seen on ferns is caused by a 'leather-leaf fern gall mite'.

Growing It: Hard to establish but grows well on rocks and walls in dry conditions. Used as ground cover and in hanging fern baskets. If transplanting, keep the growing tip above the soil surface.

Photos (top centre left): 'travelling fern moth' whose caterpillars tunnel inside the fronds.

FRONDS
SIMPLE

LIFE SIZE

19

Paretao
Strap Fern

Notogrammitis billardierei * [Family: Polypodiaceae]

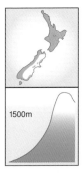

1500m

Size: Fronds 3–20 cm long

Features: Tufted perching fern. Fronds *narrow, blunt and strap-like*. Clusters of spore cases on the undersides form a *herring-bone pattern*

Where: Common in forest or scrub on the lower sections of tree trunks, on rocks and occasionally on the ground. Native to New Zealand and Australia

The spore clusters on the undersides of the fronds of this fern are arranged in parallel lines, as they also are on two spleenwort ferns that share the same Māori name, paretao, which is a kind of obsidian used for cutting, inferring perhaps that these lines look like incisions. *Notogrammitis* comes from the Greek *gramma*, also meaning lines, refering to the same characteristic feature; *billardierei* commemorates Jacques Houtou de la Billardière (1766–1834), a French explorer who studied New Zealand plants. Known in Australia as **finger fern** or **common finger-fern**.

Nature Notes: In spite of a hormonal insecticide contained on the fronds, the tiny maggot of a kind of 'fern leafminer' fly tunnels inside them. Fronds are also eaten by kererū (New Zealand pigeons).

Growing It: Impossible to cultivate and unwise to attempt transplanting.

LIFE SIZE

* Previously known as *Grammitis billardierei*.

Whare-Ngārara
Lance Fern

Loxogramme dictyopteris* [Family: Polypodiaceae]

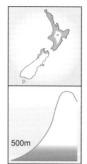

500m

Size: Fronds 7–30 cm long

Features: Creeps as a mat over tree trunks, forming small *tufts of undivided, thin, fleshy, pointed fronds.* Large brown spore-patches on the undersides of fronds (photo, above) form visible bulges on top

Where: Common on smooth-barked trees, but also on rocks and banks. Native only to New Zealand

The European name compares the simple shape of the tender green fronds with the bladed tip of a lance. Their curving shape could also be compared with that of a green gecko, suggesting an origin of the Māori name. These fronds are most often noticed on the lower trunks of trees (particularly nīkau) but they can also form an even carpet over stones, rocks and tree roots, sometimes covering quite large areas. In dry weather, the fronds hang limply against their support – a feature that distinguishes them from the young fronds of fragrant fern (page 23). Another feature that distinguishes the two is a lack of obvious side veins on the fronds of lance fern.

Nature Notes: So far, no specific insects are known to associate with this fern.

Growing It: Difficult. Needs a glass case with plenty of humus and damp, shady conditions.

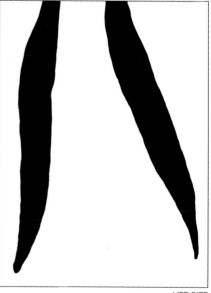

LIFE SIZE

FRONDS SIMPLE

* Previously known as *Anarthropteris lanceolata*.

21

Kōwaowao
Hound's Tongue Fern

Microsorum pustulatum * [Family: Polypodiaceae]

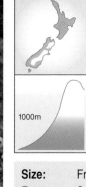

Size:	Fronds 8–70 cm long
Features:	Scrambling or climbing fern with a *thick, fleshy stem*. The long-stalked, *very glossy*, leathery fronds are strap-like when young, widening to become very deeply lobed. Underside of native frond shown below
Where:	Very common in forest and scrub on trees, rocks or dry ground. Native to New Zealand and Australia

Kōwaowao means 'to overgrow or choke'. Also known as **pāraharaha**, meaning 'a spread-out clump'. Members of the Tūhoe tribe (Urewera) cooked the young fronds in a hāngi as greens. The European name is an old one given to several overseas plants with tongue-like leaves. Australians call it **kangaroo fern**, likening the frond-shape to a kangaroo's footprint (with one long and one short toe).

Nature Notes: Kererū (pigeons), kōkako, wild pigs, goats, deer and two kinds of native fern looper caterpillar feed on the fronds, while the caterpillar of the native 'black-lyre leafroller' moth (right) hides in silken tubes on dying fronds. Maggots of a 'fern leafminer' fly tunnel inside the fronds. Caterpillars of the 'fern spore-eater moth' consume the spores. Other insects risk losing their skins due to an insect-moulting hormone, *ecdysone*.

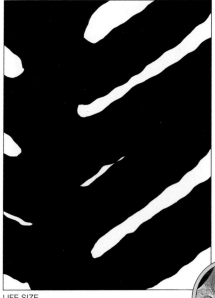

LIFE SIZE

Growing It: Can be grown with shade on dry ground, or over logs.

Photos (top): 'angled fern looper' caterpillar and moth.

* Also known as *Phymatosorus diversifolius* or *Zealandia pustulata*.

22

Mokimoki
Fragrant Fern

Microsorum scandens* [Family: Polypodiaceae]

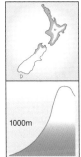

1000m

Size:	Fronds 13–60 cm long
Features:	Scrambling or climbing fern with a *wiry stem. Dull*, thin fronds, strap-like when young (left), widening and becoming deeply lobed into up to 20 pairs of leaflets, *with net-like veins.* Underside of mature frond shown above
Where:	Common in forest on trees, rocks or damp ground. Native to New Zealand and Australia

Fresh fronds smell of cut grass, but dried, they soon emit a strong and lasting, sweet, marzipan-like fragrance. These were formerly used by Māori to scent hair and body oil, for perfuming a house when guests were expected or to make sachets for wearing around the neck, and this use may be the origin of 'mokimoki' or **moki** (mōkī meaning 'packet'). (The chemistry of this perfume has not so far been investigated.)

Nature Notes: Fronds are sometimes found with tunnel-marks within from the maggot of a native 'fern leafminer' fly. On the underside of fronds, in webbing coated with spores, lives the caterpillar of a native 'fern spore-eater moth'. It bores holes through fronds, leaving towers of spores on the upper side of the frond.

Growing It: In shade, once established on damp ground with a tree to climb, but not commercially available and almost impossible to raise from spore.

* Also known as *Phymatosorus scandens* or *Dendroconche scandens*.

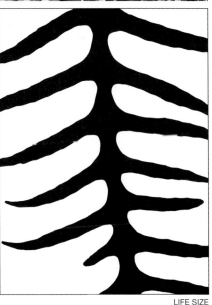

LIFE SIZE

23

Peretao
Waterfall Fern

*Blechnum colensoi** [Family: Blechnaceae]

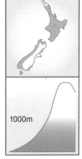

Size:	Fronds 16–60 cm long
Features:	Creeping ground fern. Dark, shiny, long-stalked fronds, undivided or divided once into a few leaflets only. These look as if they have been stamped out of a piece of leather. Spores on separate shrivelled-looking fronds
Where:	Common *hanging* along dark, *damp forest banks, especially near waterfalls*. Native only to New Zealand

A most striking fern whose fronds are most often noticed clinging to the sides of shaded waterfalls, as if stamped out of leather. Though now known to be native only to New Zealand, this fern has been confused with similar-looking ferns in the Pacific Islands, the Philippines, Malaysia, India and Australia. Also known as **peretako** or **petako**, names that associate it with the adze-like 'sickle spleenwort'. *Blechnum* ferns are unusual in that some fronds – with shrivelled, thread-like leaflets – specialise in producing spores, while others never produce spores. This feature can be a useful clue to their identification.

Nature Notes: So far, no specific insects are known to associate with this fern.

Growing It: Hard to maintain; best in very damp soil in a fairly dark place, with constant dripping water.

LIFE SIZE

* Also known as *Austroblechnum colensoi*.

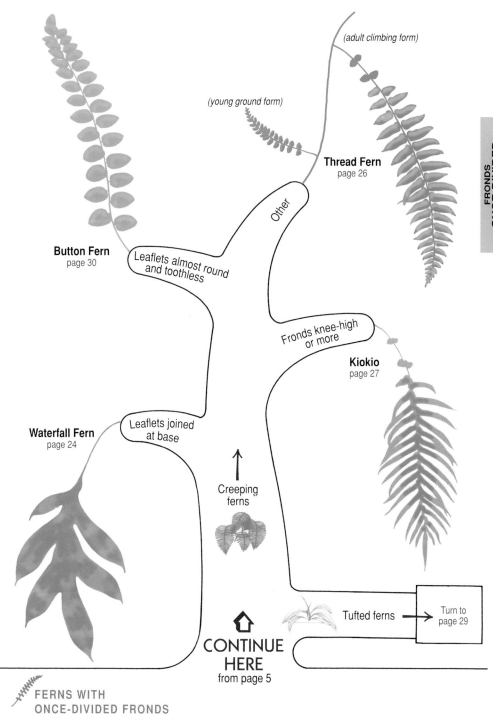

(adult climbing form)

(young ground form)

Thread Fern
page 26

Other

Button Fern
page 30

Leaflets almost round
and toothless

Fronds knee-high
or more

Kiokio
page 27

Waterfall Fern
page 24

Leaflets joined
at base

Creeping
ferns

⬆
**CONTINUE
HERE**
from page 5

Tufted ferns → Turn to
page 29

FERNS WITH
ONCE-DIVIDED FRONDS

25

Pānako
Thread Fern

*Blechnum filiforme** [Family: Blechnaceae]

A

B

Size:	Creeping fronds 6–30 cm; climbing ones up to 70 cm
Features:	Creeping and climbing fern. *Ground fronds* (B) *very small with roundish leaflets. Larger, climbing ones* (A) *have very long, pointed leaflets.* Fronds with thread-like leaflets (shown above) bear the spores
Where:	Common in forest. Native only to New Zealand

Having three quite different frond shapes makes this unique among New Zealand ferns. The name 'thread fern' refers specifically to one of these forms: the fine, wispy leaflets of fertile fronds seen overhead on the trunks of trees. These look very different from the little fronds sprawling on the ground, or the much larger climbing adult ones. Indeed, it is hard to believe they belong to the same plant. The root-like rhizomes contain *ß-sitosterol*, the main active ingredient of an American proprietary drug used to lower blood cholesterol levels. The fern's Māori name is shared with shining, and shore, spleenwort ferns.

Nature Notes: Leaflets of the ground fronds frequently show signs of having been nibbled by an unknown kind of invertebrate, possibly fern weevils.

Growing It: Difficult to propagate and not available commercially. Best in a shady, sheltered spot near a suitable tree.

LIFE SIZE

(A) Adult, climbing form
(B) Young, ground form

* Also known as *Icarus filiformis*.

Kiokio
Palm-Leaf Fern

*Blechnum novae-zelandiae** [Family: Blechnaceae]

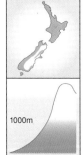

1000m

Size: Fronds 30–320 cm long

Features: Large, creeping ground fern. Leaflets strap-like and very finely-toothed. Spores on separate, rather shrivelled-looking fronds. New growth *tinged pink or red*

Where: Extremely common on road and track cuttings, gullies and cliffs, in scrub and swamps. Native only to New Zealand

Māori used fronds to wrap vegetable food to add flavour during hāngi cooking. The curled fiddleheads can also be eaten and have a mild taste that improves with cooking. The striking pinkish tinges on the new growth is caused by *flavonoids* – the fern's equivalent of sunburn cream. The Māori name suggests an association with parallel lines in tattooing or the bonefish (kiokio) of tropical Polynesia – or both.

Nature Notes: Native caterpillars of two kinds of fern looper, and two kinds of leaf-tyer moth eat the fronds. Various types of native weevil feed on fronds, spores or 'roots'. On Codfish Island, fronds and 'roots' (rhizomes) are eaten by kākāpō.

Growing It: Very hardy. Best on a bank, where its long fronds can hang to good effect. Prefers damp, shady places. Growing in pots and hanging baskets will prevent it becoming a weed. Available from nurseries. Transplants easily.

LIFE SIZE

Photo (top): 'striped fern looper' moth, whose caterpillars feed on the fronds.

*Also known as *Parablechnum novae-zelandiae*. Previously known incorrectly in New Zealand as *Blechnum capense* – an African species not found here.

Pākau
Gully Fern

*Pneumatopteris pennigera** [Family: Thelypteridaceae]

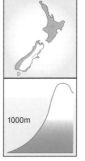

1000m

Size:	Slender trunk to waist high; fronds 35–175 cm long
Features:	Tufted ground fern, sometimes forming a short, thin trunk. The *pale, dark-veined fronds* have brown stalks, with 15–30 pairs of long, round-notched leaflets. Underside of mature frond shown above
Where:	Common in damp forest gullies. Native to New Zealand and Australia

The fronds are among those used by Māori as flavouring, tied around, placed under or over vegetable food in hāngi (earth cooking pits). Māori of the Urewera district (Tūhoe) also ate the young fronds. In the late 19th century, the scraped roots were reportedly effective as poultices for boils. Chemists have recently found four new *glycosides* in the fronds. In Tasmania it is known as **lime fern** (in reference to where the fern is most often found). Also known as **feather fern**, or, in Māori, as **pākauroharoha** ('fluttering bird wings'), or simply pākau ('wing').

Nature Notes: In autumn and winter, brown caterpillars (top left) of 'striped fern looper' moths feed on the underside of fronds.

Growing It: Not particular about soil, but needs damp, sheltered, shaded ground protected from frost. Transplants well while still small.

LIFE SIZE

* Also known as *Pakau pennigera.*

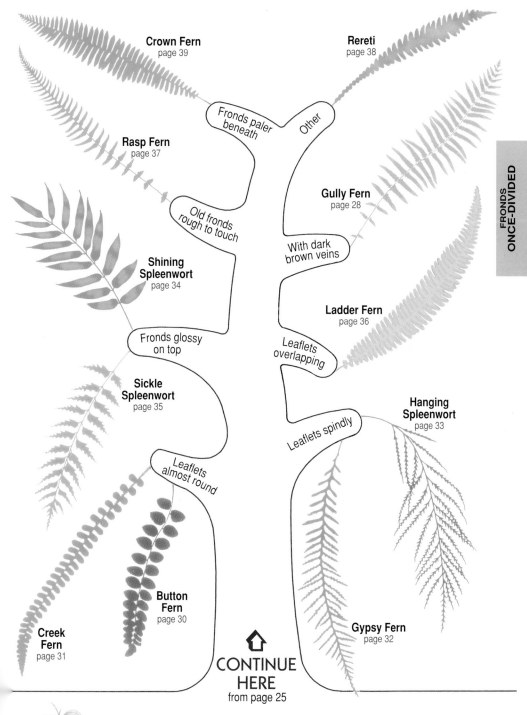

Crown Fern
page 39

Rereti
page 38

Fronds paler beneath

Other

Rasp Fern
page 37

Gully Fern
page 28

Old fronds rough to touch

With dark brown veins

Shining Spleenwort
page 34

Ladder Fern
page 36

Fronds glossy on top

Leaflets overlapping

Sickle Spleenwort
page 35

Hanging Spleenwort
page 33

Leaflets spindly

Leaflets almost round

Button Fern
page 30

Creek Fern
page 31

⬆
CONTINUE
HERE
from page 25

Gypsy Fern
page 32

TUFTED FERNS WITH
ONCE-DIVIDED FRONDS

Tarawera Button Fern

Pellaea rotundifolia [Family: Pteridaceae]

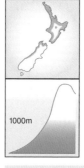

1000m

Size:	Fronds 20–60 cm long
Features:	Loosely tufted ground fern with very narrow, upright fronds on fine, dark brown stems. *Dark, shiny leaflets* on tiny stalks, widely spaced, *almost round, sometimes slightly pointed.* Underside of mature leaflets shown above
Where:	Common in forest in dry rocky places or light scrub. Native only to New Zealand

The rounded leaflets are arranged like a string of buttons on a thread-like stalk; hence the fern's common European name. The fronds were among those tested for the insecticidal compounds known as *phytoecdysones* that are found in several New Zealand native ferns. The toxic effect of the fronds of this species on the maggots of the common house-fly was amongst the highest recorded – a fact that is expected to have some commercial application.

Nature Notes: Despite their toxicity, nibbled fronds are often seen, most likely chewed by some kind of native fern weevil.

Growing It: Delicate and attractive; available from nurseries. Prefers light, rich soil. Requires a certain amount of sunlight – otherwise the leaflets tend to drop off. Also sensitive to over-watering. Popular as a house plant too, either in a pot or in a hanging fern basket.

LIFE SIZE

Kiwikiwi
Creek Fern

Blechnum fluviatile* [Family: Blechnaceae]

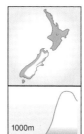

Size: Fronds 20–85 cm long

Features: Tufted ground fern. Fronds have 20–60 pairs of *almost round, olive-green*, fairly uniform-sized leaflets. Amid the dense flattish or drooping rosette of fronds stand a few upright, fertile fronds (left)

Where: Common in damp, shady forest, often by streams. Native to New Zealand and Australia

The upright, fertile fronds are reminiscent of kiwi feathers, a possible origin of the Māori name (although 'kiwa' in the alternative, **kiwakiwa**, is also a Polynesian fern name in its own right). In Australia, the ray-like arrangement of the fronds earned it the name **ray water fern**. Others have likened it to a starfish or octopus. In the late 19th century, fronds were used for what was then known as splash-work – a technique similar to modern-day spray stencilling. Fronds were chewed by Māori to alleviate sore mouths and tongues, and are known to contain a hormonal insecticide.

Nature Notes: Eaten by deer. Tiny maggots of a 'fern leafminer' fly tunnel within the fronds; fronds are also commonly notched by insects – either by native 'fern leaf beetles' or 'fern weevils'.

Growing It: Attractive and available from nurseries. Needs constant moisture, some shade and a rich, well-drained soil.

LIFE SIZE

* Also known as *Cranfillia fluviatilis*.

31

Taupeka
Gypsy Fern

*Notogrammitis heterophylla**[Family: Polypodiaceae]

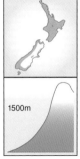

1500m

Size: Fronds 5–30 cm long

Features: Small tufted fern on rocks, trees or banks. Leaflets spindly and leathery, *the longest having deeply-jagged edges*

Where: Common, hanging from forest trees, but also (often stunted in size) on wet rocks and banks. Native to New Zealand and Australia

This fern typically hangs suspended (tau) from a branch (peka) – taupeka. The botanical name is likewise descriptive, from the Greek, *ktenos*, a comb, and *pteris*, a fern; *heterophylla* meaning 'with differing leaves'. The fronds vary a great deal from one another, but all have the appearance of a double-sided comb, hence its alternative common name, **comb fern**. In Australia it is known as gypsy fern, most likely from the remarkable range of situations in which the fern grows; it is found the length of New Zealand, from subalpine scrub and Westland rainforest to inhospitable rock crevices on Rangitoto Island.

Nature Notes: No specific insect has so far been recorded as feeding on this fern.

Growing It: Surprisingly difficult. Transplanting is not recommended.

LIFE SIZE

*Previously known as *Ctenopteris heterophylla*.

Makawe
Hanging Spleenwort

Asplenium flaccidum [Family: Aspleniaceae]

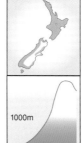

1000m

Size: Fronds 10–125 cm long

Features: Tufted *perching* fern. Fronds very distinctive; leathery, spindly and pale, usually *drooping rather limply*. Underside of mature frond shown left

Where: Common in forest, perching in trees, but also as erect tufts on the ground or rocks, even on exposed coasts. Native to New Zealand and Australia

The full Māori name, **ngā makawe o Raukatauri** means 'ringlets of hair of the goddess of music'. Also known as **drooping spleenwort** or – in Australia – as **weeping spleenwort**. All names refer to the way in which the fern hangs from trees. 'Spleenwort' (an old English name for *Asplenium* ferns generally) refers to the reputation from the 1st century AD of one species (*A. cetcrach*) that was used for treating enlarged spleens, liver and kidney complaints. (Note that 'wort' in such names is pronounced *wert*.)

Nature Notes: Fronds eaten by kōkako (top left), kererū, goats and deer. Pale squiggles visible inside some fronds are made by the tunnelling maggots of a kind of native 'fern leafminer fly'.

Growing It: Easy to transplant. Best in very rich soil, with space for the fronds to droop. Often grown in hanging baskets or pots. Don't over-water. Beware of slugs, snails and aphids.

LIFE SIZE

33

Huruhuru Whenua
Shining Spleenwort

Asplenium oblongifolium [Family: Aspleniaceae]

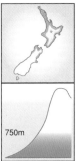

Size: Fronds 15–150 cm long

Features: Large tufted fern with very glossy fronds. Leaflets pointed with fine teeth. Brown *herring-bone pattern* on the underside of mature fronds is distinctive (see photo top left)

Where: Common on coastal cliffs, in scrub and forest, usually on ground but also on trees. Native only to New Zealand

The shiny leaves of this fern make it glow in the forest – even from a distance – as described by its Māori name, meaning 'altogether glowing'. Māori ate the young, curled shoots, which have a mild and slightly slimy taste. An attractive fern that reached the Royal Botanic Gardens at Kew in London as early as 1842.

Nature Notes: Eaten by goats and deer. The fronds are often marked by the tiny, tunnelling maggots of a 'fern leafminer fly' (top right). On the underside of the fronds, in webbing coated with spores, lives a native 'fern spore-eater moth' caterpillar, which tunnels through the frond to leave a tower of spores on the upper side. As the name suggests, caterpillars of the 'spleenwort spore-eater' moth likewise eat the spores.

Growing It: Hardy, preferring dappled sunlight. It grows either in deep leaf-mould or on old logs. An attractive basket plant, either indoors or out. Beware of slugs and over-watering.

LIFE SIZE

750m

Petako
Sickle Spleenwort

Asplenium polyodon [Family: Aspleniaceae]

FRONDS
ONCE-DIVIDED

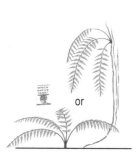

or

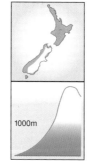

1000m

Size: Fronds 25–140 cm long

Features: Large tufted fern, usually hanging from trees. Few graceful, arching fronds, glossy above, with *shaggily and deeply toothed* leaflets. Underside of mature leaflet shown above

Where: Commonest on trees or logs in the north; on ground in the south. Native to New Zealand, Madagascar, Asia, the Pacific Islands and Australia

The original spleenwort that gave this group of ferns its name is described in Dioscorides's *De materia medica* (1st century AD) as having the power to cure enlarged spleens, as well as complaints of the liver and kidneys. 'Sickle' refers to the graceful, arching shape of the hanging fronds, while 'pere' in the alternative name **peretao** (see also page 24) is an 'adze-shaped hoe' or 'dart', tao meaning 'to weigh down'. Its unusual grace caught the attention of Victorian plant collectors inspired by the fern craze that swept England in the 1820s and 1830s. Not surprisingly, it has remained a popular fern to cultivate.

Nature Notes: Eaten by goats and deer. The leaflets are sometimes marked by the tunnelling maggots of a native 'fern leafminer fly'.

Growing It: Available in nurseries but not easy to establish. Prefers well-drained soil and dappled light. Good in a basket or as a pot plant.

LIFE SIZE

35

Ladder Fern [not native to NZ] *

Nephrolepis cordifolia [Family: Nephrolepidaceae]

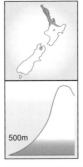

500m

Size:	Fronds 45–125 cm long
Features:	Tufted ground fern spreading by runners, with *upright*, brittle, sword-like fronds of *more than 50 pairs* of simple, toothed leaflets
Where:	Commonly grown in northern gardens, but now spreading in the wild. *Introduced* to New Zealand from the tropics

Two kinds of wild ladder fern are found in New Zealand – a native species that occurs only near hot pools in the thermal regions of the North Island, and this much more common introduced species, which is larger, glossier and widely grown in northern gardens. This common species bears small potato-like tubers that have been used for food in some countries, including Nepal. Alternative common names for it – **fishbone fern**, **herringbone fern**, **sword fern** and **tuber sword fern** – are all descriptive. (The native species lacks these tubers.)

Nature Notes: Now spreading (sometimes aggressively) in the wild.

Growing It: Best limited to indoor containers and hanging fern baskets; there is a risk otherwise of it spreading to become a nuisance. (Grows from runners and tubers in sunny, well-drained soil.) The native species remains much smaller and has similar requirements.

* This exotic fern is included here because it is so common in places that it could easily be *mistaken for a native fern*.

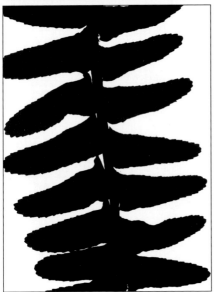

LIFE SIZE

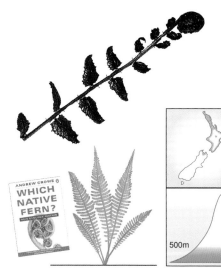

Pukupuku
Rasp Fern

Blechnum parrisiae*[Family: Blechnaceae]

Size: Fronds 15–85 cm long

Features: Tufted ground fern. Fronds *rosy-pink when young, rough and raspy when old*. New shoot shown above

Where: Commonest in the north, especially in coastal pōhutukawa forest, light scrub, tracksides and grassy hillsides – often in full sun. Native to New Zealand and Australia

The Māori name of this fern translates as 'gooseflesh' or 'goose-pimples caused by cold or fear', describing the textured surface of the fronds, as does the English name, rasp fern. The young fronds are usually pink due to the *flavonoids* they contain; these act in much the same way as sunburn cream, protecting the more delicate new growth of the fern from ultraviolet damage, thereby enabling it to thrive in full sun. The fronds also contain a powerful hormonal insecticide (an *ecdysone*) that kills the larval stages of many insects, a discovery whose commercial applications have attracted keen interest from several firms overseas.

Nature Notes: A kind of 'fern mirid' insect is found on the fronds of this and several other ferns, where it sucks the sap.

Growing It: Easy to transplant and grow. Thrives best in partial sun, where its red colouring shows the best. Sensitive to wind. Useful as a ground cover.

LIFE SIZE

*Also known as *Doodia australis* or *Doodia media* subsp. *australis*.

37

Rereti

*Blechnum chambersii** [Family: Blechnaceae]

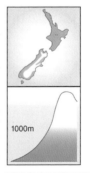

Size: Fronds 15–60 cm long

Features: Tufted ground fern, forming flattish rosettes of fronds, divided into unstalked, finely toothed leaflets. Spores on separate, rather shrivelled-looking fronds (photo, top)

Where: Common in damp forest, especially along stream banks. Native to New Zealand, Australia, possibly also Fiji, Sāmoa and Tahiti

The fronds are glossy – as described by an alternative Māori name, **nini** ('glowing'). Australians liken the frond shape to a lance, hence their name, **lance water fern**. Similarly, the name rereti, from reti, likens it to a lance or canoe. Māori collected young fronds and steamed them in hāngi pits as a form of greens. Like several other New Zealand native ferns, rereti is known to have significant insecticidal properties. The hormone involved has the power to upset developmental changes in the growth of insects but is apparently harmless to other animals, including humans.

Nature Notes: No specific insect has so far been seen feeding on the fronds.

Growing It: Grows best in conditions similar to where it is naturally found, i.e. in a damp place with plenty of shade, but a hard species to keep in an attractive condition.

LIFE SIZE

* Also known as *Austroblechnum lanceolatum*.

Piupiu
Crown Fern

*Blechnum discolor** [Family: Blechnaceae]

1000m

Size: Trunk up to waist high; fronds 25–120 cm long

Features: Tufted ground fern with an erect crown of fronds, *paler on the undersides*. Separate, rather shrivelled, erect fronds (left) bear the spores. Can also spread from runners to form colonies

Where: Common in dry, open forest. In the North Island, it is more common at high altitudes, often forming the main undergrowth in beech forest and scrub. Native only to New Zealand

The bent-over fronds have often been used as emergency track-markers, their pale undersides visible even at night. Also known as **turukio** and **petipeti**, all these common names referring to the fern's overall shape, piupiu meaning 'skirt' (think of it upside down).

Nature Notes: Though eaten by goats and deer, it is one of the few ferns to survive this and to not be browsed by possums – the latter most likely due to an unusually high concentration in young fronds of astringent-tasting tannins (over 14% by weight). Short fat grubs of a 'leaf beetle' feed on the fronds, and a native 'fern weevil' grub has been found inside the dead trunks.

Growing It: Hardy, but prefers some shade in rich, damp, well-drained soil. Small plants transplant well and grow quickly. Will grow in a container but does not flourish indoors.

* Also known as *Lomaria discolor*.

LIFE SIZE

Para
King Fern

Ptisana salicina* [Family: Marattiaceae]

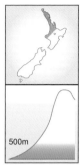

Size:	Fronds up to 4 m long
Features:	Huge, tufted ground fern, *with unusually large, heavy, dark, glossy fronds*, divided into long, strap-like leaflets. Underside of mature leaflet shown above. Stalks clasping at base, with large ear-like lobes
Where:	In heavy North Island forest. Once common, but now only in the odd, dark gully. Native to New Zealand and the South Pacific

The underground stem was an important food of Māori, inspiring an alternative name, **potato fern**. Cooked, these do taste similar to potato, but the fern is now rare and one person can eat in one day the growth of five years, so the use of wild plants nowadays as food is prohibited. 'Para' is a Polynesian term for this and related edible ferns of the tropical Pacific; alternative names, **uwhipara** and **uhipara**, liken this 'root' to that of the Polynesian white yam. The name **horseshoe fern** refers to a horseshoe-like collar at the base of the stem.

Nature Notes: Wild plants have gone from many areas due to pigs digging up rootstocks and goats eating the fronds.

Growing It: Attractive and widely cultivated. Best in rich, damp soil with plenty of shade and shelter in areas free of frost. Transplants well. Suited to growing in a tub, for either indoor or outdoor use. Hard to grow from spore.

LIFE SIZE

*Previously known as *Marattia salicina*.

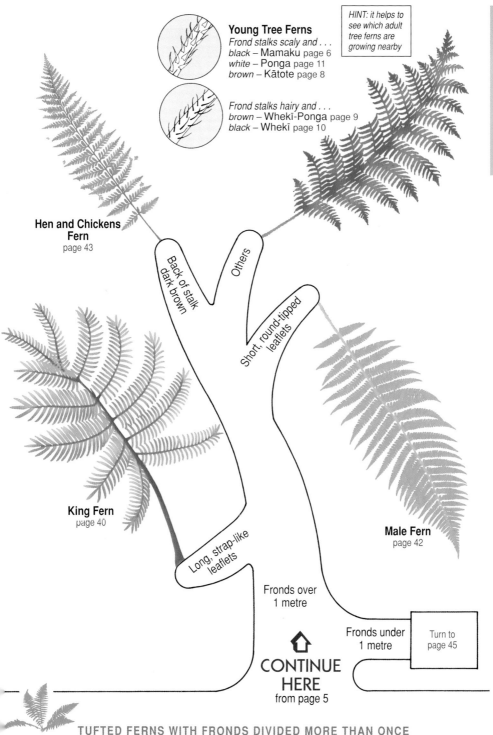

Young Tree Ferns
Frond stalks scaly and . . .
black – Mamaku page 6
white – Ponga page 11
brown – Kātote page 8

Frond stalks hairy and . . .
brown – Whekī-Ponga page 9
black – Whekī page 10

HINT: it helps to
see which adult
tree ferns are
growing nearby

**Hen and Chickens
Fern**
page 43

Back of stalk
dark brown

Others

Short, round-tipped
leaflets

King Fern
page 40

Male Fern
page 42

Long, strap-like
leaflets

Fronds over
1 metre

⌂
CONTINUE
HERE
from page 5

Fronds under
1 metre

Turn to
page 45

TUFTED FERNS WITH FRONDS DIVIDED MORE THAN ONCE

Male Fern [not native to NZ] *

Dryopteris filix-mas [Family: Dryopteridaceae]

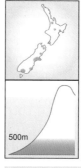

500m

Size:	Fronds 40–165 cm long
Features:	Tufted ground fern. Fronds, *paler below*. Stalk covered with wispy scales. Leaflets toothed, rounded at the end
Where:	*Introduced* to New Zealand, but spreading, particularly in waste ground and forest over much of Canterbury. Native to northern temperate countries

One of the most common ferns throughout much of Europe, Asia and North America. Its common name refers to an ancient belief that this was the male counterpart of **lady fern** (*Athyrium filix-femina*, a related fern that is likewise spreading in the Christchurch area). It is known in the old literature of Europe as **worm fern**, referring to the fact that for at least 18 centuries, the dried underground stems have been used to rid people of intestinal worms, a property this fern has due to *oleoresin*, which paralyses both the voluntary muscles of the intestine, as well as the equivalent contracting tissue of the tapeworm. In France, the shoots of this fern are boiled as a vegetable.

Nature Notes: Caterpillars of the native 'black-lyre leafroller' moth (above) hide in silken tubes on dying fronds.

Growing It: Favours moist soil under shade in a cool climate. Fronds die off in the winter. (Take care not to let this fern spread.)

* This exotic fern is included here because it is so common in places that it could easily be *mistaken for a native fern*.

LIFE SIZE

Mouku
Hen and Chickens Fern

Asplenium bulbiferum [Family: Aspleniaceae]

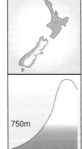

750m

Size:	Fronds 20–155 cm long
Features:	Tufted ground fern. *Stalks and midribs dark brown below, green above.* Fronds feathery, and usually recognised by *young plants growing on the upper surface* (see photo, above)
Where:	In forest throughout. Native to New Zealand and Australia

Known in Australia as **mother fern**; this and the name 'hen and chickens' refer to how young plants sprout from the fronds, taking root as the old frond drops to the ground (though the fern can also reproduce from spores in the usual way). Mouku (or **mauku**) is a general Polynesian term for herbs, grasses and ferns, many of which were used for mulching taro plants – in much the same way as these fronds were used by New Zealand Māori. Members of the Tūhoe tribe are also known to have used these fronds as mat-like bed blankets. Māori also cooked and ate the succulent young unexpanded shoots.

Nature Notes: The fern's survival is threatened in some areas by wild goats, deer and pigs. The tiny maggot of a native 'fern leafminer' fly sometimes tunnels in the fronds. Fronds also eaten by kererū.

Growing It: Easily grown from young plantlets, which is best done with part of the old frond left attached. Prefers damp humus in shade; also grows well indoors as a pot plant. Note that nursery stock is often not the native species, but an attractive hybrid.

LIFE SIZE

43

Maukurangi
Miniature Tree Fern

*Blechnum fraseri** [Family: Blechnaceae]

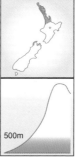

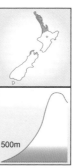

Size:	*Very slender trunk to waist high*; fronds 25–60 cm long
Features:	Fronds dark, glossy and leathery, with *triangular teeth along the central stalk.* Spores on separate, finer fronds with longer stalks
Where:	A common fern in dry forest and scrub. Native to New Zealand, Indonesia and the Philippines

'Mauku' is a general Polynesian term for herbage, 'rangi' meaning an elevated platform or tower. Although unrelated to true tree ferns, 'miniature tree fern' is nevertheless an equally good name, likening this primordial-looking plant to a bonsai version of its namesake. Its form is indeed striking, so that it comes as no surprise to find this fern in the Royal Botanic Gardens at Kew in London – one of several ferns sent there in the 1830s or 1840s by the naturalist, anthropologist and missionary, the Rev. William Colenso.

Nature Notes: Four kinds of scale insect – two of them native – live on the fronds, sucking the sap.

Growing It: Not easy to establish. However, will grow quickly in warm weather if given a fair amount of light and well-drained soil. When grown successfully, it can make an interesting groundcover. Difficult to grow from spore.

LIFE SIZE

* Also known as *Diploblechnum fraseri*.

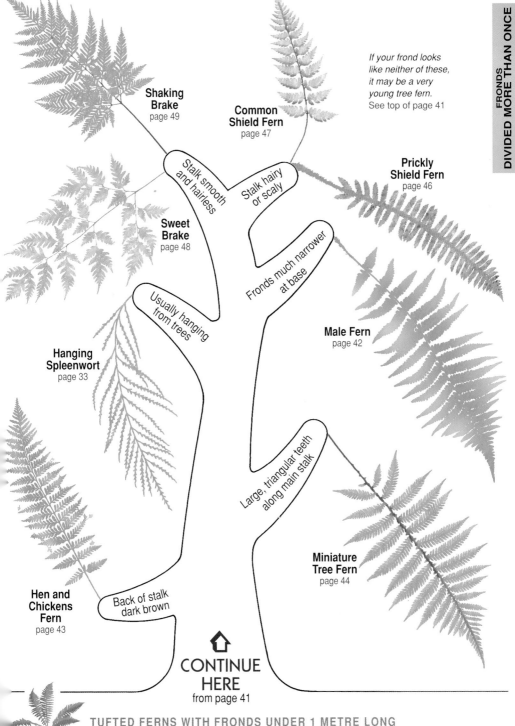

*If your frond looks
like neither of these,
it may be a very
young tree fern.*
See top of page 41

**Shaking
Brake**
page 49

**Common
Shield Fern**
page 47

**Prickly
Shield Fern**
page 46

Stalk smooth
and hairless

Stalk hairy
or scaly

**Sweet
Brake**
page 48

Fronds much narrower
at base

Usually hanging
from trees

Male Fern
page 42

**Hanging
Spleenwort**
page 33

Large, triangular teeth
along main stalk

**Hen and
Chickens
Fern**
page 43

Back of stalk
dark brown

**Miniature
Tree Fern**
page 44

⌂
CONTINUE
HERE
from page 41

TUFTED FERNS WITH FRONDS UNDER 1 METRE LONG
AND DIVIDED MORE THAN ONCE

Pūniu
Prickly Shield Fern

Polystichum vestitum [Family: Dryopteridaceae]

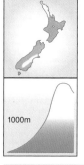

1000m

Size:	Trunk to waist high; fronds 30–150 cm long
Features:	Tufted ground fern. Its long, narrow, prickly fronds are made up of small leaflets, dark shiny above, paler below. *Stalks thick and very densely covered in large, dark scales.* Underside of mature frond shown above
Where:	In forest, scrub and tussock. Very common in the south. Native only to New Zealand

The ancestors of New Zealand Māori apparently likened the growing tuft form (pū) of this and the Prince of Wales Feather fern (page 15) to that of the coconut (niu). Gwen Skinner recommends the fiddleheads: 'They lend flavour to stews and casseroles and can be put into the pot to boil with meat – particularly beef pot roasts'. However, with so much of it being now browsed by deer and possums, it would be better to limit the fern's use to emergency survival rather than culinary garnishing.

Nature Notes: The tiny caterpillars of the 'pūniu spore-eater' moth live in silk tunnels on the underside of the fronds, eating spores, while those of the 'pale fern looper' and 'zigzag fern looper' moths feed on the fronds. A kind of native weevil grub lives in the stalks. This is one of many plants to have suffered badly from browsing by deer. Also favoured by possums.

Growing It: Not particular about shade, but likes the cold and does best in deep leaf-mould or peat. Available from nurseries.

LIFE SIZE

Pikopiko
Common Shield Fern

Polystichum neozelandicum* [Family: Dryopteridaceae]

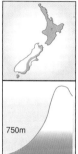

750m

Size:	Fronds 20–85 cm long
Features:	Tufted ground fern with few fronds, dark, shiny and leathery, on black, wiry stalks covered in short, hair-like scales. Underside of mature frond shown below. Coastal plants are more fleshy (see footnote)
Where:	Common in coastal areas but also inland on rocks, or ground in scrub and forest. Native only to New Zealand

The name pikopiko means 'fiddlehead', a term whose use was extended to this fern whose cooked 'fiddleheads' were eaten. These days, they are boiled with meat or bacon bones. One author recommends them cooked and served with melted butter on toast or simply as a vegetable, but they are better regarded nowadays as an emergency survival food. Also known as **pīpiko**, **tutoke** or **black shield fern**.

Nature Notes: Fronds eaten by kererū (New Zealand pigeons). The caterpillar (top right) of the 'zigzag fern looper' moth feeds on the fronds, while those of a native 'fern spore-eater moth' live on the underside of fronds in webbing coated with spores, boring holes through the frond from below to leave towers of spores on the upper side.

Growing It: Difficult to establish in gardens and hence not commercially available. Not particular about shade or soil, but will need watering in dry weather.

*Previously known as *Polystichum richardii.*

LIFE SIZE

Titipo
Sweet Brake

Pteris macilenta [Family: Pteridaceae]

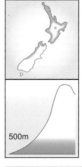

500m

Size:	Fronds 35–140 cm long
Features:	Tufted ground fern. Stems yellow-brown. *Fronds delicate and thin*, more open in appearance than shaking brake (opposite). *Teeth at tips of lobes.* Veins meet up to form a net-like pattern
Where:	Common in the north in open forest. Native only to New Zealand

Also known simply as **sweet fern**. The origin of both European names remains a mystery, for the fern neither tastes nor smells particularly sweet. Neither is there any evidence that it is greatly liked by stock. On the medicinal front, the active principle of a related overseas fern (*Pteris ensiformis*) has proven effective in curing bacillary dysentery in cases where other more conventional treatments failed. Hold a frond of sweet brake up to the light to see its characteristic net-like pattern of veins.

Nature Notes: Two kinds of specialist fern weevils feed on the spores, while the caterpillars (top left) of the 'common fern looper' moth and 'orange peel moth' (see opposite page) feed on the fronds.

Growing It: Easy under light shade in damp conditions. Well suited to growing in a container, for indoors or out. Prefers a light, friable soil with plenty of leaf-mould.

LIFE SIZE

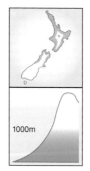

Turawera
Shaking Brake

Pteris tremula [Family: Pteridaceae]

Size: Fronds 45–150 cm long

Features: Tufted ground fern. Stems red-brown. Fronds divided into long *narrow* leaflets, harsher and less open than sweet brake (opposite). Hold a frond up to the light to check that the veins do *not* form a net-like pattern. Underside of mature frond shown above

Where: Common in the north in forest, scrub clearings and gardens. Native to New Zealand, Australia and Fiji

The English common name refers to the way this fern tends to tremble in a breeze. In summer, says one early writer, 'surveyors cutting lines through the warm sheltered gullies in which it abounds, often find the smell so strong as to be unpleasant, and I have heard it called the "stinking fern" on this account, though many people rather like the scent.' 'Wera' means 'burnt'; 'tura', 'keep clear'.

Nature Notes: Unpalatable to stock. A kind of fern weevil chews notches in the fronds (its grubs feeding on the roots); a native 'fern mirid' insect sucks the sap; and the caterpillars of the 'orange peel moth' (top) feed on the fronds.

Growing It: Very easy and fast in most soils, tolerating direct sunlight, growing well indoors. Transplants easily, but has a short life-span of about three or four years. Commonly regarded as a weed.

LIFE SIZE

Karuwhai
Climbing Shield Fern

Rumohra adiantiformis [Family: Dryopteridaceae]

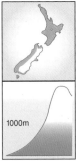

1000m

Size:	Fronds 20–85 cm long, with those growing further up the trunk often larger
Features:	Climbing fern. Fronds light with dark veins, leathery, *plastic-like* on very long, grooved stalks. *Round, jet-black spore patches* underneath mature fronds (see photo above)
Where:	Common on forest trees, especially tree ferns. Native to most southern hemisphere countries

An alternative name, **leathery shield fern**, refers to the leathery texture of the fronds and the conspicuous round, shield-like spore-case covers on the undersides of fertile fronds (see photo above). The native name suggests that Māori likened these to the eyes of a stingray (karu whai). This is one of several native ferns to contain insecticidal compounds called *phytoecdysones* that mimic developmental hormones in insects. The compound is powerful enough in small quantities to trigger inappropriate changes in the insect's growth, killing any insect unfortunate enough to try to eat it.

Nature Notes: No specific insect has so far been recorded feeding on the fronds.

Growing It: Slow and difficult to grow. Prefers cool conditions, shade and damp. Does best on a tree fern trunk, but can also look good in a hanging fern basket.

LIFE SIZE

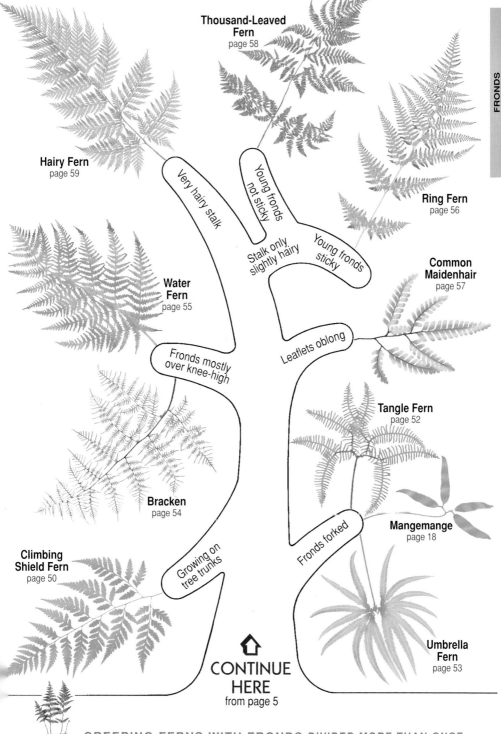

Thousand-Leaved Fern
page 58

Hairy Fern
page 59

Ring Fern
page 56

Very hairy stalk

Young fronds not sticky

Stalk only slightly hairy

Young fronds sticky

Water Fern
page 55

Common Maidenhair
page 57

Fronds mostly over knee-high

Leaflets oblong

Tangle Fern
page 52

Bracken
page 54

Fronds forked

Mangemange
page 18

Climbing Shield Fern
page 50

Growing on tree trunks

🏠
CONTINUE
HERE
from page 5

Umbrella Fern
page 53

CREEPING FERNS WITH FRONDS DIVIDED MORE THAN ONCE

Waewaekākā
Tangle Fern

Gleichenia dicarpa [Family: Gleicheniaceae]

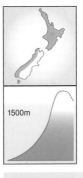

1500m

Size:	Can reach to about waist high
Features:	Creeping ground fern with *rough interlacing fronds* on erect, red-brown stalks in 1–5 tiers, each tier forked 3–5 times
Where:	Common in swampy areas and on poor soil in open scrubland. Native to New Zealand, Australia, New Caledonia, New Guinea and the Philippines

Also known as **swamp umbrella fern** – although it does also grow on dry ground. The Māori name means 'footprint of the kākā' (a large native parrot). Known in Australia as **coral fern**. With such poetic imagery, it is not surprising to find fronds used in flower arrangements. Indeed, fresh fronds of a similar and closely related fern are likewise used in Tahiti as decoration at festivals and banquets, with old stems in Malaysia serving more practical uses: sharpened to make pens, or woven into mats, partition walls, fish traps, chair seats, pouches and long-lasting caps – and even rope.

Nature Notes: The growing tips of fronds are sometimes strangled by webbing made by caterpillars of the 'Gleichenia ugly nestmaker' moth (photo above). Lumps on the underside of fronds (up to 3 mm across) are caused by the 'Gleichenia gall mite'.

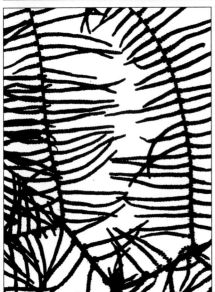

LIFE SIZE

Growing It: As in nature, tangle fern prefers poor, wet, acid soil, with a fair amount of light. Difficult to establish.

Waekura
Umbrella Fern

Sticherus cunninghamii [Family: Gleicheniaceae]

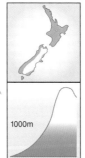

1000m

Size:	To waist high; 25–60 cm wide
Features:	Creeping ground fern with drooping, umbrella-like fronds, *whitish below*, rising in up to 3 tiers, each forking 3–4 times *in a starfish-like pattern*
Where:	Common (except in the far south) in dry open forest and roadside banks. Native only to New Zealand

Māori names liken the shape of the fronds to a parrot's footprint (wae-kura) or to the 'footprint of a white heron' (**tapuwae kōtuku**) – drawing (top, left). It is the frond's graceful, spreading shape that likewise inspired the European common name. The fronds contain small quantities of insecticidal *ecdysones*, which imitate hormones normally used by insects to initiate growth changes. This has the potential to deter many insects from feeding on the fern (although these do not affect all species in the same way).

Nature Notes: For example, the native caterpillars of the 'umbrella fern bell moth' (top right) and 'rusty umbrella fern leaf-tyer' moth continue to thrive here nonetheless, tying fronds together with webbing as safe hiding places from which to feed on the fronds.

Growing It: Hard to transplant or propagate and extremely slow-growing. One of the hardest ferns to grow and not commercially available for this reason.

LIFE SIZE

53

Rārahu
Bracken

Pteridium esculentum [Family: Dennstaedtiaceae]

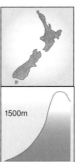

Size:	Fronds 20–400 cm long
Features:	Creeping ground fern, spreading by underground rhizomes. *Harsh fronds with smooth, chestnut-brown stems. Fiddleheads covered in fine, pale brown hairs (photo, right)*
Where:	Very common in open places. Native to New Zealand, Australia and many Pacific Islands

Also commonly known as **rahurahu** or by a Tahitian fern name, **rarauhe**; the fronds as **rauaruhe**. The prepared root-like underground stem (**aruhe**), was the most important wild vegetable food of Māori, providing a whitish starch that could be eaten alone or made into cakes sweetened with flax nectar. Correct preparation is essential since the starch and furry fiddleheads have proven to be cancer-causing when eaten raw. The hard brown frond stems were also used for making lattice fences (kākaka), kite frames and spear-like darts (teka).

Nature Notes: 'Roots' (rhizomes) dug up and eaten by kākāpō; more frequently nowadays by wild pigs. Several kinds of caterpillars, sucking bugs and weevil grubs feed on the fronds and stems. Valuable as the first stage in the succession of native forest.

Growing It: Spreads aggressively by underground stems (rhizomes). Formerly considered a major agricultural weed.

Photo (top): the introduced 'light brown apple moth'.

LIFE SIZE

Mātātā
Water Fern

Histiopteris incisa [Family: Dennstaedtiaceae]

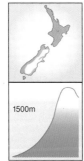

1500m

Size: Fronds 40–190 cm long

Features: Creeping ground fern. Young fronds are a distinctive *pea green, lobed like an oak leaf*

Where: In moist clearings, edges of forest and along stream banks. Native to New Zealand, and throughout tropical and southern temperate countries

The English name refers to the fact that this fern is often found near water. Likewise, the Māori name (meaning 'deep swamp'), which is applied to several other wetland plants and a wetland bird. On the other hand, Australian common names describe the frond form: **oak fern** (from the lobes of the fronds being like those on an oak leaf) and **bat's wing fern** comparing these with the spread wings of a bat. The young shoots taste exceedingly acrid.

Nature Notes: Caterpillars of the 'common fern looper' moth, 'orange peel moth' and 'golden brown fern moth' all feed on the fronds. Although the fronds are freely eaten by wild pigs and cattle, this is one of the few ferns that goats will *not* eat.

Growing It: Easy, tolerating a fair amount of sun, but preferring damp soil. Well suited to growing in a container, since it tends to spread rather too readily from underground stems. Deciduous in the south.

Photos (top, left to right): 'golden brown fern moth' and 'common fern looper' caterpillar and moth.

LIFE SIZE

Mātātā
Ring Fern

Paesia scaberula [Family: Dennstaedtiaceae]

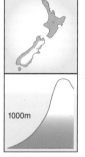

1000m

Size:	Fronds 20–115 cm long
Features:	Creeping ground fern. The fine, lacy, yellowish-green fronds are often sticky, with *zigzag* chestnut-brown stalks and a distinctive smell, especially when the sun shines on them. Underside of mature leaflets is shown above
Where:	Common on cleared, sunny, ground. Native only to New Zealand

Often seen in colonies in pasture, spreading to form an ever-increasing ring or circle – hence the name. An alternative name, **scented fern**, refers to a distinctive smell that is particularly strong when the heat of the sun has been on the fronds a while. Also appropriately known as **lace fern**. Its essential oil was investigated for perfume properties and was found to contain a *sesquiterpene* alcohol and the paraffin *n-heptacosane*. It may one day be grown as a groundcover in widely spaced stands of pine to provide compounds useful to the perfume industry. The reason for its Māori name being shared with water fern (page 55) is not clear.

Nature Notes: Tiny, whitish caterpillars of the 'ring fern spore-eater' moth (photo, top) feed on the underside of the fronds.

Growing It: Very easy in heavy soil with little shade. Not sensitive to frost. A useful groundcover.

LIFE SIZE

Puhinui
Common Maidenhair

Adiantum cunninghamii [Family: Pteridaceae]

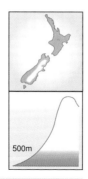

500m

Size:	Fronds 10–35 cm long
Features:	Creeping ground fern. Fronds on long, wiry, shiny, dark brown stalks. Leaflets *almost oblong, dark green above, blue-green below.* Underside of mature frond shown below
Where:	Common in coastal and lowland forest, on cliffs, banks and among mossy boulders. Native only to New Zealand

The name 'maidenhair' (for *Adiantum* ferns generally) dates back to at least the 15th century and was coined from the fine, black, hair-like stalks (left) that (according to 'The Doctrine of Signatures') inspired a belief in corresponding medicinal properties. One 17th century herbal claims that a European species 'maketh the haire [sic] of the head or beard to grow that is fallen and pulled off'. The Māori name means 'high-ranking' (nui) 'virgin' or 'topknot of hair' (puhi). This and alternative names, **huruhuru tapairu** and **makawe tapairu** (hair of the firstborn female of high rank) are early names so are not necessarily derivations from the English.

Nature Notes: Usually ignored by possums. Green caterpillars of the 'maidenhair fairy moth' and 'pale fern looper' moth are found feeding on the fronds.

Growing It: Easily grown from a clump of underground stem in shaded, moist, lime-rich soil. Not so good indoors because of its creeping habit.

Photos (top): 'maidenhair fairy moth' (male – left, and female), whose caterpillars feed on the fronds.

LIFE SIZE

57

Huarau
Thousand-Leaved Fern

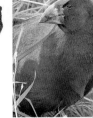

Hypolepis millefolium [Family: Dennstaedtiaceae]

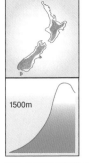

1500m

Size:	Fronds 20–100 cm long
Features:	Creeping ground fern, with open, very finely divided, hairy, wide, diamond-shaped, bright green fronds. Underside of mature frond shown above, left
Where:	Can form a striking carpet in open beech forest, especially at high altitudes. Grows right down to sea level in the south. Native only to New Zealand

The Māori name means 'abundance' (hua), 'leaf' (rau). One of New Zealand's very few deciduous native ferns and one whose summer fronds are deservedly regarded as one of the country's most beautiful. Like several native ferns, it can protect itself to some extent from insect damage by mimicking an insect-moulting hormone. This ingenious tactic makes it difficult for most insects to adapt a defence.

Nature Notes: Despite this defence, two caterpillars do feed on the fronds: those of the 'huarau looper' moth (top right) and the 'orange & purple fern looper' moth (top left). In the Fiordland winter, when the fronds have withered away, the starchy rhizomes of this fern become an important food of the now-rare takahē.

Growing It: Prefers damp, light soil and cool conditions. Not popular in cultivation since it spreads rapidly and soon dies back to look rather ragged.

LIFE SIZE

Tuakura Hairy Fern

Lastreopsis hispida [Family: Dryopteridaceae]

750m

Size:	Fronds 30–100 cm long
Features:	Creeping ground fern, with harsh, five-angled, finely divided fronds. *Stalks thickly covered in long, black bristle-like scales.* Underside of mature frond shown above
Where:	Common in forest, usually on the ground, though sometimes on tree trunks. Native to New Zealand and Australia

The Māori name for this fern was recorded in 1882 by Thomas Henry Potts and should probably read 'tūākura' (as recorded for two similar tree fern species), meaning 'moderately glowing' or 'reddish brown'. Another name, **huruhuru moho**, refers to the striking hairiness of the stem, for which the fern is known in Australia as **bristly shield fern** and informally here as 'hairy legs' (distinguishing it from a similar common New Zealand fern – *Lastreopsis glabella* – with smooth stems).

Nature Notes: In spite of the fronds containing a hormonal insecticide, caterpillars of one kind of native 'fern spore-eater moth' survive here, making webbing among spores on the underside of fronds (feeding on the spores, not on the frond itself).

Growing It: Needs shelter and damp with good drainage and only dappled sunlight. Suitable for growing in a hanging fern basket.

LIFE SIZE

59

Growing Your Own Ferns

About 50 species of New Zealand ferns are suitable for growing in the garden, most now available from plant nurseries. The key to success in growing them is to imitate as far as possible the conditions in which the fern naturally grows. A little familiarity will soon show how specialised most ferns are about the amount of shade and moisture in which they grow best, what kind of ground suits them and whether they like to grow on, or climb up, the trunks of trees. In this book you will find additional guidelines regarding their specific needs.

As a beginner, your best bet is to purchase young ferns. Transplanting from the wild may be tempting but your chances of success with most ferns are likely to be no better than 15–20%. Also, thoughtless collectors removing ferns from reserves are adding to threats to the survival of these ferns in the wild.

You may also like to try raising ferns from spores. Because ferns have no flowers, their reproduction was for centuries a complete mystery. Indeed, until the tiny dust-like spores of ferns were discovered, it was believed that ferns bore invisible, short-lived flowers only during midsummer's eve, a night credited by the prehistoric Druid religion of northern Europe as a night of mystical powers. Fortunately for fern growers, this mystery has since been solved. For, apart from having no flowers, ferns have neither fruit nor true seeds. And, while all flowering plants are either male or female or both, ferns have no gender at all.

On the underside of most fern fronds you'll find a number of dark spots or lines (*sori*). With a magnifying glass, you will find these made of many small, round bumps (*sporangia*) that contain the fern's individual, microscopic, dust-like spores.

When ripe, thousands of these spores are released and carried by the wind. Some of these that settle in a damp, shady place begin to grow – but not into ferns. Instead, they produce a tiny, heart-shaped plant about 5 mm across (a *prothallus*). This, too, has no flowers or seeds; instead, it simply has several male and female sex organs (*antheridia* and *archegonia*) that each produce lots of sperm cells and one egg.

These male and female organs mature at different times on the same plant, so the wriggling sperm have to swim over the damp surroundings (usually for no more than a couple of centimetres) until they find the egg on another sex-organ plant. The sperm fertilises this egg, which later becomes an adult fern that will replace the dying sex-organ plant. Even the giant mamaku tree fern starts life this way, from a sperm swimming across the forest floor in search of an egg.

Of course, to grow ferns from spores it helps to know all this. It is important also to know when to collect spores, how to provide the best germinating conditions and how best to sterilise containers and growing medium to keep at bay unwanted algae, fungi and insects. Though guidelines for maintaining specific ferns are given in the text, for reasons of space it is not possible here to go into more technical advice on the best methods of raising ferns from spores. For this, the best guides are Muriel Fisher's *Gardening with New Zealand Ferns* and Andrew Maloy's *Plants For Free!* (See Selected References for further details.)

Nonetheless, this little book should get you started.

Troubleshooting

First, are you sure the plant you are trying to identify is a fern?

When in the bud stage, the fronds of all common New Zealand ferns are tightly coiled like the end of a violin (a 'fiddlehead'). Most either have patches or lines of spore cases on the underside of at least some of the fronds, though some (*Blechnum* species) have instead separate, rather shrivelled-looking spore-bearing fronds.

Plants that could be confused with true ferns include two common groups of what are known as **fern allies**. These can be distinguished from ferns by their smaller leaves, unbranched veins and by their usually bearing spores on *top* of their leaves.

Fork Ferns (*Tmesipteris*)
These generally hang from the trunks of trees, especially tree ferns.

Club Mosses (*Lycopodium*)
These can hang from trees or scramble loosely over the ground.

Are you unsure whether or not it is a tree fern?

Six common ferns can produce a slender trunk, but are nevertheless NOT regarded as true tree ferns. These do not reach more than waist high, and their trunks can usually be grasped in one hand.

Crown Fern (page 39)   **Miniature Tree Fern** (page 44)   **Prince of Wales Feathers** (page 15)
Gully Fern (page 28)   **Prickly Shield Fern** (page 46)   **Single Crape Fern** (page 14)

If you have trouble matching your frond with the key:

1. Are you sure you have chosen a typical *full-grown* frond? Fronds vary a good deal in size, according to where they are growing and how mature they are.
2. Are you sure it is a *wild* fern? Garden ferns are not covered (unless they are common in the wild).
3. Are you sure the fern is *common*? Less-common ferns and those confined to special habitats (e.g., the coast, clefts in rock, bogs and around hot pools) are not included.

If the key is still not working, then take a closer look at the fern:

1. Are you sure whether it is *tufted* (with fronds clustered in a tight bunch) or *creeping* (with fronds either growing on an obvious vine or scattered along the ground in a line)? Where ferns grow densely enough to form a mat of fronds, it can take careful examination to tell the difference.
2. Are you sure whether the frond is *divided,* or just *deeply lobed*? If the division does not cut all the way to the stalk, then it is described as lobed.
3. Did you remember to start at the *bottom* of the *first* frond key (page 5)?

Selected References

Beever, James. *A Dictionary of Maori Plant Names*. Auckland Botanical Society, Auckland, 1987.

Best, Elsdon. *Forest Lore of the Maori*. Government Printer, Wellington, 1942.

Brockie, Robert. *A Living New Zealand Forest*. Bateman, Auckland, 1992.

Brooker, S. G., Cambie R. C. and Cooper R. C. *New Zealand Medicinal Plants*. Heinemann, Auckland, 1987.

Brownsey, Patrick J. and Smith-Dodsworth, John C. *New Zealand Ferns and Allied Plants*. Bateman, Auckland, 1989.

Burkill, I. H. *A Dictionary of the Economic Products of the Malay Peninsula*. 2 vols. Crown Agents for the Colonies, London, 1935.

Camus, Josephine M. et al. *A World of Ferns*. Natural History Museum Publications, London, 1991.

Chinnock, R. J. and Heath, Eric. *Common Ferns and Fern Allies* (Mobil NZ Nature Series). Reed, Auckland, 1981.

Cooper, R. C. and Cambie, R. C. *New Zealand's Economic Native Plants*. Oxford University Press, Auckland, 1991.

Crowe, Andrew. *A Field Guide to the Native Edible Plants of New Zealand*. Penguin, Auckland, 2004.

Crowe, Andrew. *The Life-Size Guide to New Zealand Native Ferns – Featuring the unique caterpillars which feed on them*. Penguin, Auckland, 2004.

Dobbie, H. B. *New Zealand Ferns*. Whitcombe and Tombs, Auckland, 1930 (and other editions).

Field, H. C. *The Ferns of New Zealand*. Willis, Wanganui, 1890.

Fisher, Muriel E. *Gardening With New Zealand Ferns*. Collins, Auckland, 1984.

Hamlin, Bruce. *Native Ferns* (Nature in New Zealand Series). Reed, Wellington, 1963.

Heath, Eric and Chinnock, R. J. *Ferns and Fern Allies of New Zealand*. Reed, Wellington, 1974.

Hutchinson, Amy. *Plant Dyeing*. The Daily Telegraph Co., Napier, 1941.

Maloy, Andrew. *Plants for Free! – A New Zealand Guide to Plant Propagation*. Shoal Bay Press, Christchurch, 1992.

Martin, R. W. *Ferns For Ferneries*. Betty Simpson, Wanganui, c 1980.

Metcalf, Lawrie. *Ferns of New Zealand*. New Holland, Auckland, 2003.

Molloy, Brian. *Ferns in Peel Forest – A Field Guide*. Dept. of Lands and Survey, Christchurch, 1983.

Potts, T. H. *Out in the Open* (includes Classified List of New Zealand Ferns). Lyttelton Times Company, Christchurch, 1882.

Russell, G. B. 'Insect Moulting Hormone Activity in Some New Zealand Ferns.' *NZ Journal of Science* 14: 31–35. March 1971.

Skinner, Gwen. *Simply Living*. Reed, Wellington, 1981.

Stevenson, Greta. *A Book of Ferns*. John McIndoe, Dunedin, 1954.

Thomson, G. M. *The Ferns and Fern Allies of New Zealand*. Henry Wise, Dunedin, 1882.

Williams, Herbert W. *A Dictionary of the Maori Language*. Government Printer, Wellington, 1985.

The ecological and chemical information in this book has mostly been gleaned from specialist journals including *Australian Journal of Chemistry, New Zealand Journal of Botany, New Zealand Journal of Zoology, Notornis*, various standard bird reference books, private communications with specialist entomologists and the Crop & Food Research invertebrate herbivore – host plant association Plant-SyNZ™ database: **http://plant-synz.landcareresearch.co.nz**

For the origins of Māori names, I owe much to the work of Bruce Biggs, including 'A Linguist Revisits the New Zealand Bush' (in Pawley, A. (Ed.) *Man and a Half: Essays in Pacific Anthropology and Ethnobiology in Honour of Ralph Bulmer*. Memoir No. 48: 67–72. The Polynesian Society, Auckland, 1991); and his unpublished work, *The Comparative Polynesian Lexicon Project* (POLLEX). My own small contribution is from a larger referenced project that stems from research into Polynesian languages, entitled *Pathway of the Birds: The Voyaging Achievements of Māori and their Polynesian Ancestors* (Bateman, 2018). You will find more information on the Māori fern names used in this book, including sources for these on page 4.